SRA Imagine It!

Skills Practice
Workbook

**Level 1
Book 2**

McGraw Hill · **SRA**

Columbus, OH

SRAonline.com

 SRA

Send all inquiries to this address:
SRA/McGraw-Hill
4400 Easton Commons
Columbus, OH 43219-6188

ISBN: 978-0-07-610475-8
MHID: 0-07-610475-3

7 8 9 QLM 13 12 11 10

The McGraw-Hill Companies

Table of Contents

Unit 7 **I Think I Can**

Unit 8 · Away We Grow!

Unit 9 Home, Sweet Home

Unit 10 I Am Brave

Name _____ **Date** _____

Sounds and Spellings

OW

Practice Write the words and sentence in the spaces provided. Write a rhyming word to finish the last sentence.

how _____   now _____

Take a towel to the shower.

_____

_____

_____

A cow that was <u>brown</u> went to the _____.

Apply   **Write the word described by each picture.**

| cat   cow   crow | shower   tower   flower |

_____
- - - - - - - - - - -
_____

_____
- - - - - - - - - - -
_____

Dictation

_____
- - - - - - - - - - - - - -
_____

_____
- - - - - - - - - - - - - -
_____

_____
- - - - - - - - - - - - - -
_____

_____
- - - - - - - - - - - - - -
_____

Name _____ **Date** _____

Writing a Make-Believe Story

Think   **Audience: Who** will read your story?

_____

Purpose: What do you want your make-believe story to do?

_____

_____

Prewriting   **Plan your make-believe story using the story map below.**

Who is the main character?

↓

What is your main character's problem?

Do any other characters help or cause the problem?

↓

How does your character solve his or her problem?

Revising   **Use this checklist to revise your make-believe story.**

☐ Is the problem presented at the beginning and a solution at the end of the story?

☐ Did you add descriptive details or dialogue?

☐ Did you revise your story with a partner?

Editing/Proofreading   **Use this checklist to correct mistakes.**

☐ Are all words spelled correctly?

☐ Did you use correct capitalization and punctuation?

☐ Do quotation marks appear before and after all dialogue phrases?

Publishing   **Use this checklist to get your report ready to share.**

☐ Copy your story on a clean sheet of paper.

☐ Draw illustrations to go with your story.

☐ Present your story to the class in a creative way.

Name _____ **Date** _____

Sounds and Spellings

ou_

Practice **Write the words and sentence in the spaces provided.**

_____   _____

out _____   house _____

A mouse ran out.

_____

_____

_____

The cloud is round.

_____

_____

_____

Apply | **Write the word that correctly completes each sentence.**

| house | out | flower | found | sound | frown |

1. The clown had a _____ on his face.

2. The brown _____ is big.

3. Amber _____ her mitten.

4. The player was _____ at home plate.

5. A rose is Mom's favorite _____.

6. The kids did not make a _____.

Name _____ **Date** _____

Quotation Marks

Rule

Quotation marks are used at the beginning and end of the exact words someone says. They show what characters say in a story.

Example

"I want to go to the store," said Mary.

Practice **Read each sentence. Underline the exact words someone says. Circle the name of the speaker.**

1. "There's a red starfish clinging to that rock," said Andy.

2. Dad pointed and said, "Look at all the tiny fish!"

3. "Watch out for that hermit crab!" laughed Tanya.

Apply — **Read the sentences. Write quotation marks at the beginning and end of the exact words someone says.**

4. Let's make a sand fort! said Tanya.

5. Andy asked, Where can we make it?

6. This looks like a good spot, said Tanya.

7. Andy smiled and said, I'll make the towers.

8. We work well together, said Tanya.

Name _____ **Date** _____

Sounds and Spellings Review

Practice **Write the word on the line that correctly names each picture.**

> flour   bounce   clown
> sprouts   owls   trout

1. _____

2. _____

3. _____

4. _____

5. _____

6. _____

Apply   **Write the word that best completes each sentence.**

| flowers | hound |
| around | outside |

7. Murphy is a nice _____.

8. Sometimes he just sits _____ on the porch.

9. Then he walks _____ the yard and smells

the _____.

Dictation

Name _____ **Date** _____

Selection Vocabulary

Focus

meadow (med' · ō) *n.* a grassy field (p. 16)

kite (kīt) *n.* a toy that flies in the sky on a long string (p. 16)

Practice **Circle the correct word that completes the sentence.**

1. Alex's _____ flew high in the sky.

   a. carry   **b.** stop   **c.** kite

2. Two cows ate grass in the _____.

   a. meadow   **b.** music   **c.** today

Apply Tell whether the boldfaced definition given for the underlined word in each sentence below makes sense. Circle Yes or No.

> meadow   kite

3. The <u>meadow</u> was filled with flowers.

    running . . . . Yes   No

4. It is not too windy to fly your <u>kite</u>.

    a toy that flies in the sky on a long string. . . . . Yes   No

5. We ate a picnic lunch in the <u>meadow</u>.

    grassy field . . . . Yes   No

6. Gina's yellow <u>kite</u> looks pretty in the blue sky.

    quickly . . . . Yes   No

Name _____ **Date** _____

/ow/ spelled *ow* and *ou_*

Focus

Rule	Examples
The /ow/ sound can be spelled *ow* or *ou_*.	town gown ouch slouch

Word List
1. crown
2. tower
3. pouch
4. outside
5. allow
6. chowder
7. round
8. mouse

Challenge Words
9. flower
10. playground

Practice Sort the spelling words under the correct heading.

/ow/ spelled *ow*

1. _____

2. _____

3. _____

4. _____

/ow/ spelled *ou_*

5. _____

6. _____

7. _____

8. _____

Apply   **Write the spelling word next to its meaning clue.**

9. a small bag to carry things _____

10. to permit _____

11. a structure that is
higher than its surroundings _____

12. a small rodent with long tail _____

Circle the correct spelling for each word.
Write the correct spelling on the line.

13. croun   crown _____

14. rownd   round _____

15. outside   owtside _____

16. chouder   chowder _____

Name _____ **Date** _____

Alphabetical Order

Rule

Alphabetical order, or **ABC order,** means that a group of words is put in the same order as the letters of the alphabet.

Example

apple   bat   cat   dog

Practice

Write the following words on the lines in alphabetical order.

cloud   town   baker   monkey   zipper

1. _____

2. _____

3. _____

4. _____

5. _____

Apply **Rewrite each group of words on the lines so that they are in ABC order.**

Group 1

yes
pig
game

Group 2

puzzle
happy
taller

6. _____

7. _____

8. _____

9. _____

10. _____

11. _____

Name _____ **Date** _____

Sounds and Spellings

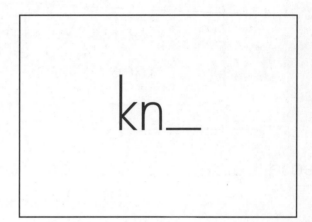

kn_

Practice **Write the words and sentences in the spaces provided.**

_____   _____

knit _____   knot _____

I know that knight.

_____

_____

Sue knows how to knit.

_____

_____

Apply **Write the word that best completes each sentence.**

| know knock |
| knee knot knead |

1. Please _____ on the window.

2. She wondered how to tie a _____.

3. Do you _____ how to skate?

4. Grandma showed me how to _____ the batter.

5. He hurt his _____ playing football.

Name _____ **Date** _____

Cause and Effect

What makes an event happen is called the **cause.** The event that happens is the **effect.**

Read each effect. Circle the best cause, either a or b.

1. Jake put ice cubes in a glass.
   a. He wanted to empty the ice tray.
   b. He wanted a cold drink of water.

2. Our class went to the cafeteria.
   a. It was lunchtime.
   b. We needed practice walking in the hallways.

3. The frog snapped at the fly.
   a. It didn't like bugs.
   b. It was hungry.

Apply **Read each effect. Draw a line to match it to its cause.**

4. John ran home from the park.

   a. There was a breeze blowing.

5. The grass was very tall.

   b. Her old shoes were too small.

6. Beth bought new shoes.

   c. They were going to build a house.

7. Anna closed all the windows.

   d. She was going on a trip.

8. Pam packed her bags.

   e. He was late for dinner.

9. Men made stacks of lumber.

   f. No one had mowed it.

Name _____ **Date** _____

Sounds and Spellings

aw

au_

Practice **Write the words and sentences in the spaces provided.**

raw _____ bawl _____

pause _____

The baby crawls on the lawn.

_____

_____

_____

Apply   **Write the word from the box that completes each sentence.**

1. Paul put milk in the _____.

2. The hawk raised its _____.

3. Mom made _____ to put over the pasta.

saw

saucer

straw

claw

sauce

shawl

Name _____ **Date** _____

Writing a Make-Believe Story

Think **Audience: Who** will read your story?

_____

_____

Purpose: What do you want your make-believe story to do?

_____

_____

Prewriting **Use the story map below to help plan your make-believe story.**

Beginning:

↓

Middle:

↓

End:

Revising **Use the following checklist to revise your make-believe story.**

☐ Does your story have a beginning, middle, and end?

☐ Did you describe your story's setting?

☐ Did you use details like description and action words in your story?

Editing/Proofreading **Use the following checklist to check your writing for mistakes.**

☐ Are all words spelled correctly?

☐ Did you use correct punctuation, including quotation marks?

☐ Did you use singular and plural nouns and pronouns correctly in your story?

Publishing **Use this checklist to prepare your story for publication.**

☐ Copy your story on a clean sheet of paper.

☐ Use a fun way to present your story like dressing up as a character.

Name _____ **Date** _____

Sounds and Spellings

> **aw** as in w**a**lk and b**all**

Practice **Write the words and sentences in the spaces provided.**

stalk _____   wall _____

small _____   chalk _____

You should always walk in the hall.

_____

_____

_____

_____

Apply **Circle the correct word that completes each sentence. Write the word on the line.**

I. I need to _____ to my mother.

talk   tall

2. Matt and Jeff _____ to the park.

wall   walk

Dictation

_____   _____

_____   _____

_____   _____

_____

Name _____ **Date** _____

Singular and Plural Pronouns

Focus

Rule
We use **pronouns** to replace nouns and make writing easier and more interesting to read.

Example
Dawn has pretty hair.
She has pretty hair.

Practice **Read the sentence. Look at the picture. Write the correct pronoun on the line.**

it   they   we   he   him   she   I

1. I can kick _____ very far.

2. _____ is on my team.

3. _____ is my coach.

Apply **Read each pair of sentences. Write the correct pronoun in the blank.**

she   he   her   them   I

4. My name is Kim.

_____

_____ am seven years old.

5. Janet likes to paint.

_____

_____ is an artist.

6. Chad lives next door.

_____

_____ likes to draw.

7. Janet and Chad are going to an art show.

_____

I am going with _____.

Name _____ **Date** _____

Sounds and Spellings

> **aw** as in c**augh**t and th**ough**t

Practice **Write the word on the line that completes each sentence.**

> bought   taught   ought
> brought   thought

1. Dawn and I think our dog _____
   to have a new doghouse.

2. We _____ it would be fun to make it.

3. We _____ some wood and nails.

4. Mr. Hon _____ over his tools.

5. He _____ us how to make the doghouse.

Apply **Read the clues. Write the word in the puzzle.**

thoughtful caught fought daughters

Across

3. did catch

4. very kind

Down

1. argued

2. what girls are to their parents

Name _____ **Date** _____

/aw/ spelled *au_* and *aw*

Focus

Rule	Examples
The /aw/ sound can be spelled *au_* and *aw*.	law fawn cause

Practice **Sort the spelling words under the correct heading.**

/aw/ spelled *au_*

1. _____

2. _____

3. _____

4. _____

/aw/ spelled *aw*

5. _____

6. _____

7. _____

8. _____

Word List
1. draw
2. lawn
3. fault
4. auto
5. saw
6. pause
7. awful
8. because

Challenge Words
9. applaud
10. straw

Apply Circle the correct spelling for each word. Write the correct spelling on the line.

9. drau   draw   _____

10. becawse   because   _____

11. lawn   laun   _____

12. auful   awful   _____

Write the spelling word next to its meaning clue.

13. a short break   _____

14. mistake   _____

15. a car   _____

16. pictured with the eye   _____

Name _____ **Date** _____

Sounds and Spellings Review

Practice **Write the word that names the picture.**

> chalk   crawl   straws   launch   faucet   hawk

1. _____   2. _____

3. _____   4. _____

5. _____   6. _____

Apply **Unscramble the words and write the sentence correctly.**

7. dawn. fawn wakes up The at

_____

- -

_____

Dictation

_____   _____

- - - - - - - - - - - - - -   - - - - - - - - - - - - - -

_____   _____

- - - - - - - - - - - - - -   - - - - - - - - - - - - - -

_____   _____

- - - - - - - - - - - - - -   - - - - - - - - - - - - - -

_____

- - - - - - - - - - - - - -

_____

Name _____ **Date** _____

Selection Vocabulary

Focus

> **dining car** (dīn´ · ing kär) *n.* a room on a train where meals are served and eaten (p. 54)
>
> **fine** (fīn) *adj.* very nice (p. 54)
>
> **yards** (yärdz) *n.* a place for railroad cars (p. 62)
>
> **riddles** (rid´ · əlz) *n.* Plural of **riddle:** a question or problem that is hard to solve (p. 73)

Practice **Write the word that completes each sentence.**

1. We ate lunch in the _____ of the train.

2. My brother has a book of jokes and _____.

3. Maria saw ten blue railroad cars in the _____ downtown.

4. It was a _____ sunny day.

Apply Draw a line to match each word on the left to its definition on the right.

5. yards

a. very nice

6. dining car

b. places for railroad cars

7. fine

c. questions or problems that are hard to solve

8. riddles

d. a room on a train where meals are served and eaten

Name _____ **Date** _____

Sounds and Spellings

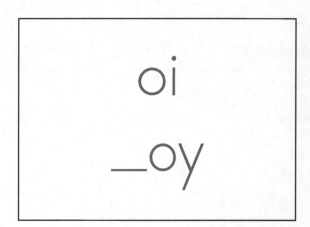

oi

_oy

Practice **Write the words and the sentence on the lines provided.**

_____   _____

noise _____   joy _____

The boy has a nice voice.

_____

_____

_____

Apply **Complete each sentence with the correct word from the box.**

coins toy noise moist point

1. He got a _____ at the store.

2. The pencil has a _____.

3. She collects _____.

4. The loud _____ woke us.

5. The muffin was soft and _____.

Dictation

_____ _____

_____ _____

_____ _____

_____ _____

Name _____ **Date** _____

Writing a Biography

Think **Audience: Who** will read your biography?

_____

_____

Purpose: What do you want your biography to do?

_____

_____

Prewriting **Plan your biography using the web below.**

Revising Use the following checklist to revise your biography.

☐ Did you add details so the reader knows more about the person?

☐ Did you use describing and action words in your biography?

Editing/Proofreading Use the following checklist to check your writing for mistakes.

☐ Did you use correct spelling and punctuation, including quotation marks?

☐ Did you use possessive nouns and pronouns correctly in your writing?

Publishing Use this checklist to prepare your biography for publication.

☐ Copy your biography on a clean sheet of paper.

☐ Use a fun way to present your biography like dressing up as the person, or adding illustrations to your writing.

Name _____ **Date** _____

Sounds and Spellings Review

Practice   **Write the word that names each picture.**

> hoist   toys   oil   coins   cowboys   coil

1. _____

2. _____

3. _____

4. _____

5. _____

6. _____

Apply Write the word on the line that correctly completes each sentence.

> enjoyed voice choice annoyed
> noise boiled loyal spoiled

7. What was that strange _____?

8. Troy must make a _____ about which book to read next.

9. Mom threw the _____ milk in the garbage.

10. Joyce has a nice singing _____.

11. Dad _____ some corn for dinner.

12. Roy _____ his trip to the beach.

13. The playful puppy _____ the old dog as it tried to sleep.

14. Leroy and Joy are _____ friends.

Name _____ **Date** _____

Possessive Pronouns

Rule	**Example**
Possessive pronouns take the place of possessive nouns. Possessive pronouns show ownership.	Laura has a blue shirt. It is **her** shirt.

Practice **Read each sentence. Circle the correct possessive pronoun and write it on the line.**

1. I live in a house on Maple Street.

_____

---------------- house is green.

My   Its

2. Grandma is bringing a puppy.

_____

---------------- name is Max.

Her   Its

Apply Look at the picture. Read the sentence. Write the possessive noun and what is owned.

my   your   her   his   its

3. Maria has a book. _____

4. Ken has a ball. _____

5. The cat has a tail. _____

6. I have a balloon. _____

7. You have an apple. _____

Name _____ **Date** _____

Sounds and Spellings

 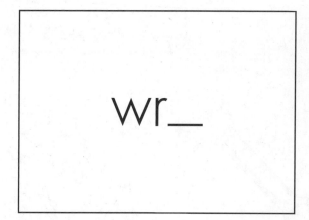

wr__

Practice Write the words and the sentence on the lines provided.

_____ _____
- -
wrist _____ wrap _____

Robots wrestle rakes.
_____
- -
_____

Apply **Write the word that goes with each picture.**

| write | wrench | wrist |

  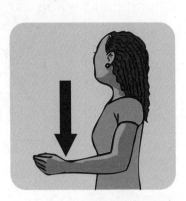

_____ _____ _____

Dictation

Name _____ **Date** _____

/oi/ spelled _oy and *oi*

Word List

1. boy
2. join
3. enjoy
4. loyal
5. spoil
6. voice
7. annoy
8. point

Challenge Words

9. voyage
10. appoint

Focus

Rule	Examples
The /oi/ sound can be spelled _oy and *oi*.	toy royal boil coil

Practice **Sort the spelling words under the correct heading.**

/oi/ spelled _oy   /oi/ spelled *oi*

1. _____   5. _____

2. _____   6. _____

3. _____   7. _____

4. _____   8. _____

Apply **Circle the correct spelling for each word. Write the correct spelling on the line.**

9. join   joyn   _____

10. poynt   point   _____

11. annoy   annoi   _____

12. loyal   loial   _____

Write the spelling word next to its meaning clue.

13. used to speak   _____

14. to damage   _____

15. to like   _____

16. a male child   _____

Name _____ **Date** _____

Selection Vocabulary

Focus

dew (dōo) *n.* moisture from the air that forms drops on the grass (p. 90)

silky (sil' • kē) *adj.* soft and smooth (p. 92)

pace (pās) *n.* the speed of walking or running (p. 100)

Practice **Write the word from the word box that completes each sentence.**

1. This morning the grass was wet with _____.

2. The baby went to sleep on a _____ blanket.

3. Dave set a fast _____ for the runners.

Apply **Write the word from the word box that matches each definition below.**

dew   silky   pace

4. _____ the speed of walking or running

5. _____ soft and smooth

6. _____ moisture from the air that forms drops on the grass

Name _____ **Date** _____

Sounds and Spellings

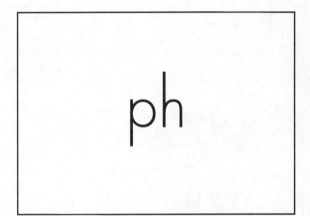

Practice **Write the words and the sentence on the lines provided.**

_____   _____

photo _____   trophy _____

Phil's nephew plays the saxophone.

_____

_____

_____

_____

Apply **Write the word that names each picture.**

trophy   elephant   dolphin   gopher

Name _____ **Date** _____

Sequence

Telling the events of a story in order is **sequence.**
Sequence helps readers better understand what is happening.

Practice

Look at the picture. Place the numbers 1–3 on the lines in front of the sentences to tell the correct order.

_____ They walked to the park.

_____ Then it was time to walk back home.

_____ Kelsey took the leash off the hook.

Apply **Look at the picture. Read the sentences. Write First, Next, Then, and Finally on the lines to tell the correct order of the story.**

_____ they reach the river where they get a drink of water.

_____ the cub wakes up and stretches.

_____ the mother tiger leads her cub through the tall grass.

_____ the mother tiger nudges her sleeping cub.

Name _____ **Date** _____

Sounds and Spellings

er as in **ear**ly

Practice **Write the word that correctly names each picture.**

earth   pearl   search   learn   early

1. _____   2. _____   3. _____

4. _____   5. _____

Apply   **Write the word on the line that correctly completes each sentence.**

| research   earns   earth   learning   heard |

6. Earl likes _____ new things.

7. Earl went to the library to do

_____

_____.

8. Earl knows that there are many different continents

_____

on _____.

9. He has _____ about some great places.

10. Earl saves the money he _____ so he can take

a trip.

Phonics • *Skills Practice 2*

Sounds and Spellings

Name _____ Date _____

| Long **ē** sound as in donk**ey** |

Practice **Unscramble the letters to spell the word that correctly names each picture.**

1.

e k y

_____

2.

e o k c y h

_____

3.

y a l l e

_____

4.

n m e o y

_____

5.

e y j r e s

_____

6.

o h n y e

_____

Apply **Choose the word that correctly completes each sentence and write it on the line.**

7. Beekeepers gather _____.

valley   honey

8. Carley got a new _____.

bee   volleyball

9. Sheep eat grass in the _____.

honey   valley

Dictation

_____   _____

_____   _____

_____   _____

Name _____ **Date** _____

Selection Vocabulary

Focus

stomped (stompt) *v.* Past tense of **stomp:** to walk heavily; to stamp with one foot (p. 117)

rather (rath′ · ûr) *adv.* more gladly (p. 117)

Practice Review the vocabulary words and definitions from *Winners Never Quit.* Write two sentences that use each of the vocabulary words.

1. _____

_____

_____

2. _____

_____

_____

| Apply | **Write the word from the word box that completes each sentence.** |

rather   stomped

3. Abby _____ around in the tall grass.

4. Would you _____ have milk or water to drink?

5. Cara is going now, but Amy would _____ go later.

6. Lee _____ on the ground with his foot.

Name _____ **Date** _____

Expanding Sentences with Describing Words

Rule
You can **expand sentences** and make them more interesting by adding **describing words.** Longer sentences have more information, such as more details and better descriptions of people, places, things, and events.

Practice **Look at the picture. Read the sentence. Use the words in the word box to help you write three longer sentences.**

plump long orange brown

fluffy pink little black

green leafy big floppy

The bunny eats a carrot.

_____

_____

_____

_____

_____

Apply   **Choose one of the lunchboxes. Read the sentence. Write three longer sentences using describing words.**

I have a new lunchbox.

_____

- -

_____

- -

_____

- -

_____

- -

_____

_____

_____

Name _____ **Date** _____

Sounds and Spellings Review

Practice | **Name the pictures. Find and circle the word in the puzzle. Write the word on the line.**

```
p   h   b   g   u   e   a   r   t   h   z
e   e   a   r   t   h   w   o   r   m   s
a   k   a   t   u   r   k   e   y   s   d
r   r   e   a   r   n   i   n   g   s   l
l   y   m   o   n   k   e   y   s   f   e
s   s   e   o   c   h   i   m   n   e   y   s
```

Clues

1. _____ 2. _____ 3. _____

4. _____ 5. _____ 6. _____

Apply Read each riddle. Write the word from the word box that correctly answers each riddle.

> hockey   learn   earth   donkey

7. I may be math.

I may be reading.

I am what you do every day.

What am I?

_____

- - - - - - - - - - - - - - - - -

_____

8. I am an animal.

I carry things and people.

I look like a horse.

What am I?

_____

- - - - - - - - - - - - - - - - -

_____

9. I am a sport.

Players wear ice skates.

Players move a puck on ice.

What am I?

_____

- - - - - - - - - - - - - - - - -

_____

10. I am a planet.

I am where you live.

I have land and water.

What am I?

_____

- - - - - - - - - - - - - - - - -

_____

Name _____ **Date** _____

/er/ spelled *ear* and /ē/ spelled *_ey*

Focus

Rule
One way to spell the /er/ sound is: *ear.* The vowel sounds of the letters e and a are controlled by the letter *r.* One way /ē/ can be spelled is *_ey.*

Examples
yearn   monkey

Word List
1. earth
2. money
3. honey
4. heard
5. donkey
6. search
7. learn
8. valley

Challenge Words
9. unheard
10. volleyball

Practice **Sort the spelling words under the correct heading.**

/er/ spelled *ear*   /ē/ spelled *_ey*
_____   _____

1. _____   5. _____

_____   _____

2. _____   6. _____

_____   _____

3. _____   7. _____

_____   _____

4. _____   8. _____

Apply   **Write the spelling word next to its meaning clue.**

9. land surface

_____

10. a horse-like animal

_____

11. a food made by bees

_____

12. low land between hills or mountains

_____

Circle the correct spelling for each word.
Write the correct spelling on the line.

13. money   mone

_____

14. heard   hird

_____

15. search   serch

_____

16. lern   learn

_____

Name _____ **Date** _____

Interviewing

One way to find out about a person is through an **interview.** If you asked someone questions to find information for your biography, you conducted an interview. Before doing an interview, it is good to prepare a list of questions to ask.

Practice **Who will you interview from your class?**

_____

- -

_____

Below are some questions that might be helpful to ask in an interview.

1. When were you born?

2. Where were you born?

3. Where did you go to school?

4. What is your favorite subject in school?

5. Why is this your favorite subject?

Apply Conduct an interview with someone in your class. Write questions in the space provided and record the answers from your partner.

_____

- -

_____

- -

_____

- -

_____

- -

_____

- -

_____

Use the space below to take more notes while you are conducting your interview.

Name _____ **Date** _____

Timed Writing

Think   **Audience: Who** will read your timed writing?

_____

Purpose: What do you want your timed writing to do?

_____

_____

Prewriting   **Follow these steps for timed writing.**

1. Read the entire prompt. Circle the directions for writing the paper.

2. Underline each thing you are asked to write about.

3. Reread each reminder.

4. Make notes about what you will write. Spend only a few minutes making notes.

5. Write your paper!

6. Check to make sure you did each reminder.

7. Revise as needed.

Revising **Use this checklist to make your timed writing better.**

☐ Did you complete each reminder?

☐ Does your writing stay on topic?

☐ Are your sentences clear?

Editing/Proofreading **Use this checklist to check your writing.**

☐ Did you begin every sentence with a capital letter?

☐ Did you use correct end marks?

☐ Are all words spelled correctly?

Name _____ **Date** _____

Changing Sentences

Focus You can **begin sentences** in different ways to make your writing more interesting.

Practice Read each telling sentence, and then rewrite it so it becomes an asking sentence. The first word of the sentence is given for you.

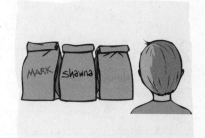

1. Our class is going on a field trip.

Is _____

2. We are going to an aquarium.

Where _____

3. Some parents will come with us.

Who _____

Apply **Rewrite each telling sentence so that it is an asking sentence.**

I. Grandpa gave Ted a puppy.

_____

- -

_____

2. Ted named his new puppy Dusty.

_____

- -

_____

3. Dusty looks like a black fluffy ball.

_____

- -

_____

4. Ted takes Dusty for a walk every day after school.

_____

- -

_____

5. Ted and Dusty are good pals.

_____

- -

_____

Name _____ **Date** _____

Sounds and Spellings Review

Practice Draw a line to match the picture to the correct word. Write the word on the line.

1. pant

2. wax

3. paint

4. grass

5. bat

6. wakes

7. bait

_____
_____
_____
_____
_____
_____
_____

Apply **Write the correct word to complete the sentence. There will be one word that you do not use. Write it at the bottom of the page.**

| jacket   flat   painted   badge   latch   track   tank |

1. Dan had his car _____ for the big race.

2. He puts on his racing _____.

3. He attaches the _____ he must wear.

4. Dan makes sure the _____ is full of gas.

5. He checks to see that the tires are not _____.

6. Cars begin dashing around the _____.

What word did you not use? _____

Name _____ Date _____

Selection Vocabulary

Focus

aside (ə•sīd)
adv. to one side
(page 159)

root (ro͞ot) *n.* part of a plant that grows down into the ground (page 157)

Practice   **Review the vocabulary words and definitions from "How a Seed Grows." Write a sentence using each vocabulary word.**

1. _____

_____

_____

2. _____

_____

_____

Apply **Write the word from the word box that completes each sentence.**

aside   root

1. A _____ grows from a seed.

2. The soil is pushed _____ by the growing root.

3. The _____ of a plant draws water from the soil.

4. Please move _____ to let others on the bus.

Name _____ **Date** _____

Long a spelled *a_e* and *ai_*

Focus

Rule	Examples
Long vowels sound like their names. Two ways long a can be spelled are *a_e* and *ai_*.	pave save bait sail

Practice

Sort the spelling words under the correct heading.

long *a* spelled *a_e*

1. _____
2. _____
3. _____
4. _____

long *a* spelled *ai_*

5. _____
6. _____
7. _____
8. _____

Word List

1. snake
2. aim
3. tape
4. pale
5. wait
6. trail
7. rain
8. wave

Challenge Words

9. trailer
10. snakeskin

Apply   **Next to each word, write the spelling word that rhymes.**

9. make _____

10. bait _____

11. mail _____

12. sale _____

Circle the correct spelling for each word.
Write the correct spelling on the line.

13. rane   rain _____

14. aim   ame _____

15. taip   tape _____

16. waiv   wave _____

Name _____ **Date** _____

Writing a Book Report

Think   **Audience: Who** will read your book report?

_____

_____

Purpose: What do you want your book report to do?

_____

_____

Prewriting   **Use the story map to plan your book report.**

Beginning

Middle

End

Revising **Use this checklist to make your book report better.**

☐ Does your paragraph stay on topic?

☐ Did you move words to make your book report clear?

☐ Are there words you can add to tell more about your book?

Editing/Proofreading **Use this checklist to check your book report.**

☐ Did you use pronouns correctly?

☐ Did you use correct end marks?

Publishing **Use this checklist to get your book report ready to share.**

☐ Copy your book report on a clean sheet of paper.

☐ Create a book jacket or illustrate a scene from the book to go with your book report.

Name _____ **Date** _____

Plural Possessive Pronouns

Rule
A **plural possessive pronoun** shows ownership. It takes the place of a noun that means more than one.

Example
This cat belongs to us. This cat is **ours.**

Practice | **Complete each sentence with the correct plural possessive pronoun.**

| our | ours | their | theirs | your | yours |

1. That house across the street belongs to us.

_____

It is _____ house.

2. Mandy and Rick planted a garden.

_____

_____ garden has many plants.

Apply   **Read each sentence. Choose the correct possessive pronoun from the box. Write it on the line.**

| mine | your | his | her | their | hers | our |

Grandma has a big attic. There are three old trunks in

_____

_____ attic. Inside the trunk I found a picture of

_____

Mom and Dad. It was _____ wedding picture.

These old ice skates would fit Grandma. They must be

_____

_____.

Name _____ **Date** _____

Sounds and Spellings Review

Practice   Write the word on the line that has the same vowel sound as the picture.

| spine   might   mit   twine   dries   twin   pickle   knit |

1. _____

2. _____

3. _____

4. _____

5. _____

6. _____

7. _____

8. _____

Apply **Write the correct word on the line that completes each sentence.**

| sniff | tries | kitten |
| climb | nibbles | hides |

9. We have a _____ named Cricket.

10. She likes to _____ flowers in the garden.

11. She will _____ up tree trunks.

12. Cricket _____ her food.

13. She _____ to catch tiny bugs.

14. Cricket _____ under the ivy to take a nap.

Name _____ **Date** _____

Drawing Conclusions

When you read, use what you learn about the characters and events to **help you better understand the selection.**

Read the paragraph. Circle the letter that best answers each question.

Tom pushed the cart as Dad read the list. They had lettuce, celery, and cucumbers in the cart. All they needed were some tomatoes.

I. Where are Tom and Dad?

   a. at the movies

   b. at the market

   c. at the park

2. What are Tom and Dad going to make?

   a. cookies

   b. meatloaf

   c. salad

Apply **Listen as your teacher reads the story. Answer each question with an *X*. Follow the directions under each question.**

It was a hot sunny day. Mike, Sarah, and Jake laughed as they walked home together. They stopped and laid their bats, mitts, and caps on the grass. Then they sat down on the grass under a tree. It felt cool in the shade. Sarah smiled as she said, "Our team is the best!"

3. How did the children feel?

___ sad   ___ happy   ___ disappointed   ___ angry

Draw a circle around the words that tell you this.

4. What had the children been doing?

___ playing soccer   ___ swimming

___ playing baseball   ___ playing tag

Draw two lines under the words that tell you this.

5. Did they win?

___ yes   ___ no

Draw a box around the words that tell you this.

Name _____ **Date** _____

Long i spelled *i_e* and *_y*

Word List
1. fine
2. time
3. dry
4. shy
5. fly
6. mice
7. by
8. quite

Challenge Words
9. tired
10. crying

Focus

Rule	Examples
Two ways long i can be spelled are *i_e* and *_y*.	kite dime pry my

Practice **Sort the spelling words under the correct heading.**

long i spelled *i_e*

1. _____
2. _____
3. _____
4. _____

long i spelled *_y*

5. _____
6. _____
7. _____
8. _____

Apply Below each word, write the spelling words that rhyme.

nine
_____

cry
_____

9. _____

13. _____
_____

nice
_____

14. _____

10. _____

15. _____

dime
_____

16. _____

11. _____

kite
_____

12. _____

Circle the correct spelling for each word. Write the correct spelling on the line.

17. quite   quyte   _____

18. fine   fyne   _____

19. drie   dry   _____

20. shy   shie   _____

Name _____ **Date** _____

Completing a Web

Focus Filling in a **web** can help you organize information.

Practice **Read the words in the middle circle. Read the example in the oval. Add additional examples to complete the web.**

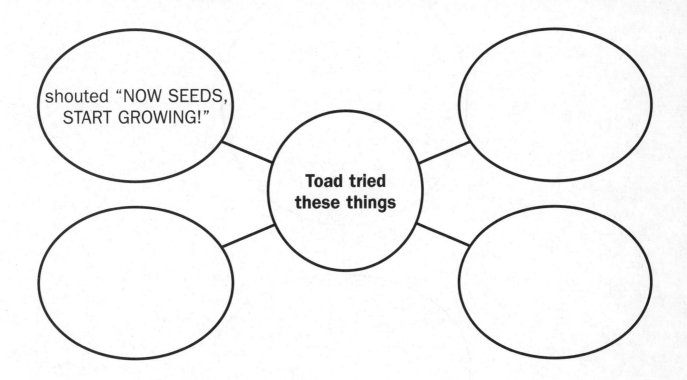

shouted "NOW SEEDS, START GROWING!"

Toad tried these things

Apply Choose something about plants you are interested in. Write it in the middle circle. Then complete the web with additional information.

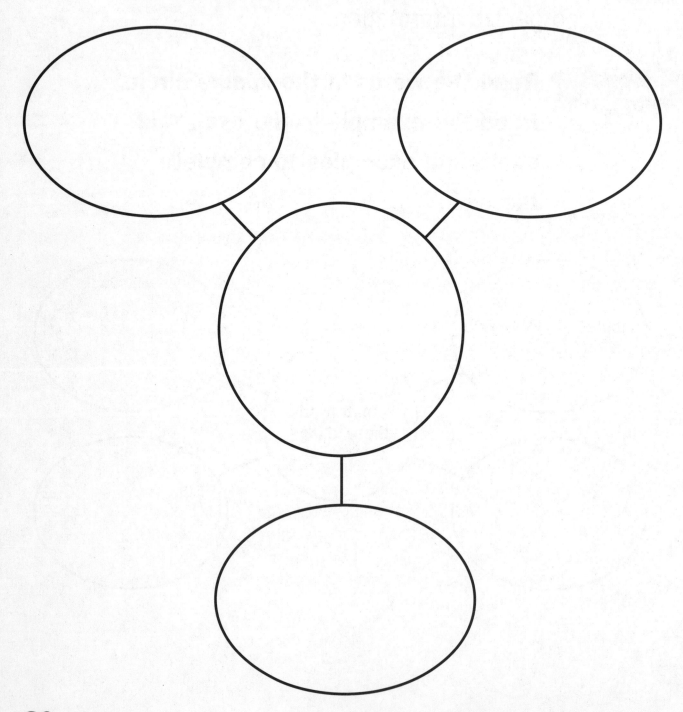

Study Skills • *Skills Practice 2*

Name _____ **Date** _____

Selection Vocabulary

Focus

flower (flou´•ûr) *n.* colored blossom (page 175)

quite (kwīt) *adv.* very (page 175)

shouted (shout´•ed) *v.* Past tense of **shout**: to call loudly (page 178)

tight (tīt) *adj.* held firmly; secure (page 196)

Practice **Write the word from the box above that matches each definition below.**

1. _____ very

2. _____ to call loudly

3. _____ held firmly

4. _____ a colored blossom

Read each sentence. Then read the definition. See if the underlined word in the sentence matches the definition. Circle Yes or No.

5. Emma planted the <u>flower</u> seeds in a pot she made at school.

   held firmly, secure . . . . Yes   No

6. We will have to go <u>quite</u> soon.

   very . . . . Yes   No

7. My brother <u>shouted</u>, "It's time to eat!"

   to call loudly . . . . Yes   No

8. The football player kept a <u>tight</u> hold on the ball.

   know . . . . Yes   No

Name _____ **Date** _____

Explaining a Process

Audience: Who will read your writing?

_____

_____

Purpose: What do you want your writing to do?

_____

_____

Prewriting **Use the sequence map to plan and organize your ideas.**

First

[   ]

Next

[   ]

Then

[   ]

Last

[   ]

Revising   **Use this checklist to make your writing better.**

☐ Are all the steps in the right order?

☐ Does each step have a time and order word?

☐ Is your title clear?

Editing/Proofreading   **Use this checklist to check your writing.**

☐ Did you begin every sentence with a capital letter?

☐ Did you use correct end marks?

☐ Are all words spelled correctly?

Publishing   **Use this checklist to get your writing ready to share.**

☐ Copy your writing on a clean sheet of paper.

☐ Draw a picture or find a photo to go with each step.

Name _____ **Date** _____

Selection Vocabulary

Focus

shrub (shrub) *n.* a bush (page 205)

vine (vīn) *n.* a plant that has a very long stem; can grow along the ground or up a wall (page 205)

stems (stemz) *n.* plural of **stem**: the stalk of a flower (page 211)

energy (e´•nər•jə) *n.* the strength to do something (page 219)

Practice **Match each word on the left to its definition on the right.**

1. shrub

a. plural of stem; the stalk of a flower

2. energy

b. a plant that has a very long stem

3. vine

c. a small tree or bush

4. stems

d. the strength to do something

Apply   **Circle the correct word that completes the sentence.**

5. Mom went outside to water the _____.

    a. shrub   **b.** sleep   **c.** little

6. There were four flowers with four long _____ in the vase.

    a. stems   **b.** energy   **c.** jump

7. Alex saw a _____ growing up the trunk of a very tall tree.

    a. five   **b.** open   **c.** vine

8. We get _____ from the food we eat.

    a. think   **b.** energy   **c.** quite

Name _____ **Date** _____

Synonyms

Practice

Read each sentence. Write a synonym for the underlined word.

1. Tanzer is a <u>large</u> black cat.

   _____

   - - - - - - - - - - - - - - -

   _____

2. He <u>jumps</u> up when he sees a butterfly.

   _____

   - - - - - - - - - - - - - - -

   _____

3. Tanzer tries to <u>grab</u> it.

   _____

   - - - - - - - - - - - - - - -

   _____

leaps

big

catch

Apply   **Read each word on the cat dish or fish. Write a synonym for the word on the line below the picture.**

> grab   crunchy   sack
> hurry   under   beautiful

1.  bag

_____

_____

2.  take

_____

_____

3.  pretty

_____

_____

4.  below

_____

_____

5.  crispy

_____

_____

6.  rush

_____

_____

Name _____ Date _____

Sounds and Spellings Review

Practice Write the word that names the picture. Then write two more words that rhyme with that word.

> rope   toast   mop   sock

1.  _____ _____ _____

2.  _____ _____ _____

3.  _____ _____ _____

4.  _____ _____ _____

Apply Read the riddle. Write the word that correctly answers the riddle. You will not use all of the words.

office   doll   phone   frog   poem   fox   bolt   yo-yo

1.
I am an animal.
I live in the forest.
I belong to the dog family.
What am I?

_____

2. I can be long or short.
I am made up of words.
You can write me.
You can read me.
What am I?

_____

3. I have many meanings.
I can be a lot of fabric.
I can be a flash of lightning.
I can hold things together.
What am I?

_____

4. I am in your home.
You can hold me.
I have buttons you push.
You use me to talk to people.
What am I?

_____

5.
I am a toy.
I have a string attached to me.
I go up, down, and around.
What am I?

_____

6. I am a place to work.
I have a desk.
I am a room.
I have supplies.
What am I?

_____

Name _____ **Date** _____

Classify and Categorize

Focus As you read, **classify and categorize** by grouping together things and ideas that are alike to help you better understand the selection.

Practice Read the category names in the box. Then read the words in each list. Write the name of the category that best describes the list of words. You will not use all of the names.

> Containers   Sports   Sounds   Plants   Tools

1. _____

   tree
   fern
   bush
   flower

2. _____

   football
   ice skating
   soccer
   softball

Apply **Read each category. Choose words from the box that belong in each group. Write the words on the lines.**

sandals   cracker   foil   book   stove   newspaper
knife   carrot   food   gold   socks   pencil

3. Things to Read

_____
_____
_____

4. Sharp Things

_____
_____
_____

5. Crunchy Things

_____
_____
_____

6. Things for Your Feet

_____
_____
_____

7. Shiny Things

_____
_____
_____

8. In the Kitchen

_____
_____
_____

Name _____

Date _____

/ō/ spelled o_e and oa_

Focus

Rule	Examples
Long vowels sound like their names. Two ways /ō/ can be spelled are o_e and oa_.	dome robe boat road

Word List

1. home
2. rope
3. toad
4. coast
5. stove
6. roam
7. goat
8. code

Challenge Words

9. lonely
10. cloak

Practice   **Sort the spelling words under the correct heading.**

/ō/ spelled o_e

1. _____
2. _____
3. _____
4. _____

/ō/ spelled oa_

5. _____
6. _____
7. _____
8. _____

Apply **Write a spelling word on the line that rhymes with each word.**

9. foam _____

10. dome _____

11. load _____

12. moat _____

Write the spelling word next to its meaning clue.

13. a cord or line _____

14. land next to the sea _____

15. a system of symbols or letters _____

16. used for cooking or heating _____

Name _____ **Date** _____

Writing a Summary

Think   **Audience: Who** will read your summary?

_____

_____

Purpose: What do you want your summary to do?

_____

_____

Prewriting   **Use the story map to plan your summary.**

Beginning:

Middle:

End:

Revising

Use this checklist to make your summary better.

☐ Did you include the most important ideas?

☐ Did you make some sentences longer?

☐ Did you write the title and author's name at the top of your paper?

Editing/Proofreading

Use this checklist to check your summary.

☐ Did you begin every sentence with a capital letter?

☐ Did you begin the title and author's name with capital letters?

☐ Did you use correct end marks?

Publishing

Use this checklist to get your summary ready to share.

☐ Copy your summary on a clean sheet of paper.

☐ Draw a picture to go with your summary.

Name _____ **Date** _____

Antonyms

Rule
Antonyms are words that mean the opposite or nearly the opposite of another word.

Example
in ⟶ out

Practice

Read each word. Choose an antonym from the box that goes with the word. Write it on the line.

| found   rude   dull   shut |

1. sharp _____

2. open _____

3. lost _____

4. polite _____

Apply   **Read each sentence. Write the antonym for the underlined word.**

> cool   short   light   down

1. It was a <u>warm</u> summer day.

_____

- - - - - - - - - - - - - - - - - -

_____

2. My family went for a <u>long</u> hike.

_____

- - - - - - - - - - - - - - - - - -

_____

3. We hiked <u>up</u> a rough trail.

_____

- - - - - - - - - - - - - - - - - -

_____

4. Each of us carried a <u>heavy</u> backpack.

_____

- - - - - - - - - - - - - - - - - -

_____

Grammar, Usage, Mechanics • *Skills Practice 2*

Name _____ **Date** _____

Sounds and Spellings Review

Practice Write the word from the word box that means almost the same thing as the word next to each number.

> smudge   human   stumble
> shrub   cube   crunch

1. tumble _____

2. bush _____

3. smear _____

4. chew _____

5. block _____

6. person _____

Apply **Read the sentences and circle the words with the short u or long u sound. Write each word under the correct column at the bottom of the page.**

It was time for lunch. Huey was hungry. He looked at a menu and ordered a sub sandwich. When the sub came, it was huge!

short _u_

_____

_____

_____

long _u_

_____

_____

_____

Name _____ **Date** _____

Compare and Contrast

Focus To help you better understand as you read, **compare and contrast** ideas, characters, and events.

Practice **Read the words in the box. Choose words that describe only a carrot and only celery. Then write the words that describe both.**

> vegetable   grows above ground   grows under ground
> healthy   green   crunchy   orange   grows from seeds

Carrot

_____

- - - - - - - - - - - - - - -

_____

- - - - - - - - - - - - - - -

_____

Celery

_____

- - - - - - - - - - - - - - -

_____

- - - - - - - - - - - - - - -

_____

Both

_____   _____

- - - - - - - - - - - -   - - - - - - - - - - - -

_____   _____

- - - - - - - - - - - -   - - - - - - - - - - - -

_____   _____

Apply **Read the story. Choose words from the box that describe each pet. Then write words that describe both.**

> girl   eight weeks old   short brown hair
> long white hair   playful   boy   puppies

Ben just brought home two new pets. They are both eight-weeks old. They love to play with Ben. Cosmo is a boy. He has short brown hair. Sassy is a girl. She has long white hair.

Cosmo

_ _

_ _

_ _

Sassy

_ _

_ _

_ _

Both

_ _

_ _

_ _

Name _____ **Date** _____

Long u spelled *u* and *u_e*

Focus

Rule	**Examples**
Long vowels sound like their names. Two ways long u can be spelled are **u** and **u_e**.	uniform tube

Word List
1. human
2. unit
3. fuel
4. music
5. mute
6. cube
7. huge
8. fumes

Challenge Words
9. unite
10. amuse

Practice   **Sort the spelling words under the correct heading.**

long u spelled *u*

1. _____

2. _____

3. _____

4. _____

long u spelled *u_e*

5. _____

6. _____

7. _____

8. _____

Apply **Circle the correct spelling for each word. Write the correct spelling on the line.**

9. music   moosic   _____

10. unet   unit   _____

11. fuems   fumes   _____

12. muet   mute   _____

Write the spelling word next to its meaning clue.

13. great size   _____

14. used to produce heat or power   _____

15. a solid shape with six equal sides   _____

16. a person   _____

Name _____ **Date** _____

Selection Vocabulary

Focus **petals** (pet´•əlz) **bright** (brīt) *adj.*
n. Plural of colorful (page 250)
petal: colored leaves
of a plant (page 235)

Practice **Write the word from the word box that completes each sentence.**

1. The _____ flowers grew
in pots outside the store.

2. Roses have pretty _____.

3. The _____ of the
daisy are long and white.

4. An artist used many _____ paints to make
that picture.

Apply **Review the vocabulary words and definitions from "Flowers" and "Flowers at Night." Write a sentence using each vocabulary word.**

bright   petals

5. _____

6. _____

Name _____ **Date** _____

Writing a Summary

Think **Audience: Who** will read your summary?

_____

_____

Purpose: What do you want your summary to do?

_____

_____

Prewriting **Use the web to plan your summary.**

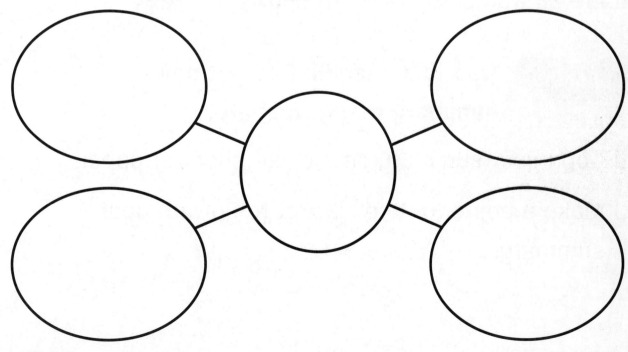

Revising · Use this checklist to make your summary better.

☐ Did you include the most important ideas?

☐ Did you write sentences of different lengths?

☐ Did you include contractions when appropriate?

Editing/Proofreading · Use this checklist to check your summary.

☐ Did you begin the title and author's name with capital letters?

☐ Did you use correct end marks?

☐ Are all words spelled correctly?

Publishing · Use this checklist to get your summary ready to share.

☐ Copy your summary on a clean sheet of paper.

☐ Make a poster or book jacket to go with your summary.

Name _____ **Date** _____

Selection Vocabulary

Focus

trapping (trap´•ing) v. allowing entrance but no exit (page 260)

wetlands (wet´•landz) n. land consisting of marshes and swamps (page 261)

attracts (ə•trakts´) v. draws attention to (page 262)

insects (in´•sekts) n. Plural of **insect:** a six-legged bug with a three-part body and no backbone (page 262)

Practice **Write the vocabulary word that completes each sentence.**

1. Many animals make their home in _____.

2. Some plants can get food by _____ bugs.

3. The sweet smell of roses _____ bees.

4. _____ sometimes are eaten by plants.

Apply **Write the word from the word box that matches each definition below.**

| trapping | wetlands | attracts | insects |

5. _____ marshes and swamps

6. _____ a bug with six legs

7. _____ allowing entrance but no exit

8. _____ draws attention to

Name _____ **Date** _____

Contractions

Rule
A **contraction** puts two words together. Some letters are left out. An apostrophe (') shows where the letters are missing.

Examples
do not ⟶ **don't**
you will ⟶ **you'll**

Practice On the skateboard, write the contraction for the two words above the wheels.

I'm   doesn't   it's   they'll   we're

1. they   will
_____

2. I   am
_____

3. we   are
_____

4. it   is
_____

Apply **Read each sentence. Write the contraction for the underlined words.**

5. It is such a hot day. _____

6. Dad said he will barbecue. _____

7. He can not find his cooking tools. _____

8. Look, they are in a box on the shelf. _____

9. The burgers will not get burnt. _____

10. You are a great cook, Dad! _____

Name _____ **Date** _____

Sounds and Spellings Review

Practice **Read the sentence. Rewrite the sentence using a word that means the opposite of each underlined word.**

| open | tame | follows | tiny | likes | night | stays |

I. Rudy is a <u>large</u> <u>wild</u> cat.

_____

_____

2. Rudy <u>hates</u> <u>closed</u> doors.

_____

_____

3. He <u>leads</u> me to his food dish every <u>morning</u>.

_____

_____

4. Rudy <u>leaves</u> when we have visitors.

_____

_____

Apply **Read the clue. Write the word in the puzzle.**

reuse   telescope   grinder
cider   music   California

Across

1. To use again

3. A state on the west side
   of the United States

Down

2. A tool to help see far
   away

3. A drink made from
   apples

4. Sounds that make a tune,
   or notes on a page

5. A tool that chops food

Name _____ **Date** _____

/ī/ spelled _ie
/ō/ spelled _ow

Focus

Rule	Examples
Long vowels sound like their names. /ī/ can be spelled _ie. /ō/ can be spelled _ow.	fried bow

Practice

Sort the spelling words under the correct heading.

Word List
1. tie
2. grow
3. low
4. cried
5. pie
6. throw
7. lie
8. know

Challenge Words
9. window
10. dried

/ī/ spelled _ie   /ō/ spelled _ow

_____   _____

1. _____   5. _____

_____   _____

2. _____   6. _____

_____   _____

3. _____   7. _____

_____   _____

4. _____   8. _____

Apply — Below each word, write the spelling words that rhyme.

die

9. _____

10. _____

11. _____

fried

12. _____

row

13. _____

14. _____

15. _____

16. _____

Look at each word below. Write the spelling word that is part of the same word family.

17. tied _____

18. throws _____

19. pies _____

20. knows _____

Spelling • *Skills Practice 2*

Name _____ **Date** _____

Writing a Report

Think   **Audience: Who** will read your report?

_____

_____

Purpose: What do you want your report to do?

_____

_____

Prewriting   **Write your topic in the center of the word web. Gather facts about that topic and write the facts on the word lines.**

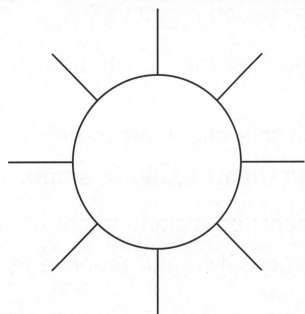

Revising **Use this checklist to revise your report.**

☐ Have you included all the facts from your word web?

☐ Did you use proofreading marks to make revising easier?

☐ Did you add details to your report to make it better?

☐ Did you delete information that does not belong?

Editing/Proofreading **Use this checklist to correct mistakes.**

☐ Have you used the present and past tense of verbs correctly?

☐ Are all words spelled correctly?

☐ Did you revise your report with a partner?

Publishing **Use this checklist to get your report ready to share.**

☐ Copy your report on a clean sheet of paper or write it on the computer. Give your report a title.

Name _____ **Date** _____

Present and Past Tense Verbs

Verbs show action. You add *—ed* to a verb to show that something has already happened.

Read each sentence. Circle the verb. Then draw an X on the line under the correct column to tell if the verb is present or past tense.

	Present	Past
1. Dad enjoyed our soccer game last week.	_____	_____
2. Polar bears play in the water.	_____	_____
3. Yesterday we wrapped gifts for grandpa.	_____	_____
4. Chad sprinkles glitter on his picture.	_____	_____
5. Aunt Mia cooks great waffles.	_____	_____
6. Mom dressed the baby in warm clothes.	_____	_____

Apply Read each sentence. Circle the correct verb and write it on the line.

1. Travis _____ hard to finish his model airplane.

   work   worked

2. Yesterday, Dana _____ many seeds in her garden.

   plants   planted

3. The bunny _____ out of its pen last night.

   hops   hopped

4. The neighbors _____ their house last month.

   paint   painted

5. They always _____ to the soccer coach before the game.   listen   listened

6. The people _____ when the show was over.

   clap   clapped

Name _____ **Date** _____

Sounds and Spellings Review

Practice Read each word. Write the word in the correct column to tell if the e has the long or short sound.

> sleepy   tread   reason
> meter   speckled   heading

Short e

1. _____

2. _____

3. _____

Long e

1. _____

2. _____

3. _____

Apply **Read the story. Write the correct word to complete each sentence.**

fell	cheered	season	speedy	even	loudly
team	field	pep	fence	bench	ended

This was the last game for the _____.

Our _____ sat on the _____

in the dugout. Coach Greer gave us a

_____ talk. The game was almost over and the score was

_____. Then Steven hit the ball over the _____.

It _____ in the _____. Steven was

_____ and made a home run. The game

_____! We jumped up and down

and _____ _____.

Name _____ **Date** _____

Selection Vocabulary

Focus

packed (pakt) *adj.* filled tightly (page 22)

clay (klā) *n.* soft, sticky mud (page 24)

roof (ro͞of) *n.* the outer covering of the top of a house or building (page 23)

sturdy (stûr´•dē) *adj.* strong (page 22)

Practice **Write the word from the word box that completes each sentence.**

1. Some bricks are made of _____.

2. The _____ of the house kept out the rain.

3. Sticks and _____ mud can make a strong house.

4. The cat climbed up the _____ tree.

Apply **Draw a line to match each word on the left to its definition on the right.**

5. roof
a. soft, sticky mud

6. packed
b. strong

7. sturdy
c. the outer covering of the top of a house or building

8. clay
d. filled tightly

/ē/ spelled *ea* and *ee*

Name _____ **Date** _____

Focus

Rule	Example
Long vowels sound like their names. Two ways /ē/ can be spelled are *ea* and *ee*.	d**ea**l m**ee**t

Word List
1. bead
2. seal
3. feet
4. greet
5. bee
6. tree
7. leak
8. flea

Challenge Words
9. teacup
10. meeting

Practice **Sort the spelling words under the correct heading.**

/ē/ spelled *ea*

1. _____
2. _____
3. _____
4. _____

/ē/ spelled *ee*

5. _____
6. _____
7. _____
8. _____

Apply **Write the spelling word next to its meaning clue.**

9. a wingless insect _____

10. an insect that gathers nectar and pollen _____

11. to welcome in a friendly way _____

12. to close up something _____

Look at each word below. If the word is spelled correctly, write the word *correct* on the line. If the word is misspelled, write the correct spelling on the line.

13. trea _____

14. leak _____

15. fet _____

16. beed _____

Name _____ **Date** _____

Irregular Past Tense Verbs and Past Tense Verbs Ending in *y*

Focus

Rule	Examples
• Some spellings of verbs change to show that something has already happened. Those verbs do not use an –*ed*.	We **sing** the song today. We **sang** the song yesterday.
• Verbs that end with a *y* change when you add an –*ed*. The **y** changes into an *i* and the **–ed** is added.	Katie tries to **hurry.** Katie **hurried** to catch the bus.

Practice **Read each sentence. Circle the verb. Then draw an X under the correct column to tell if the verb is present or past tense.**

Present   Past

1. My sweater shrank in the dryer. _____ _____

2. Chuck studied hard for his math test. _____ _____

Apply **Read each sentence. Circle the correct word and write it on the line.**

3. Dad _____ the campfire an hour ago.

    lights   lit   lighted

4. Yesterday, Margo _____ her paper neatly.

    copies   copy   copied

5. Missy _____ to school late yesterday.

    comes   come   came

6. The play _____ an hour ago.

    begins   began   beginning

7. Dad and Ted _____ the dishes last night.

    dried   dry   drying

8. We _____ new sneakers last weekend.

    buy   bought   buying

Name _____ **Date** _____

Sounds and Spellings Review

Read each sentence. Circle the word with the blend. Write the blend on the line at the end of the sentence.

1. The puppy curled up in the soft blanket. _____

2. We celebrated our team's victory. _____

3. Anna promised to be on time. _____

4. A tiny muskrat dashed under the bush. _____

5. We walked up the crooked path. _____

6. She only had time to glance at the newspaper. _____

7. We bought red flowers. _____

Apply   **Read the story. Write the word that correctly completes each sentence.**

> stopped   froze   snow
> grasped   streets   slowly

Last night was so cold that ice _____ on the

_____. Patty and Jake walked _____ down

the _____ covered sidewalk. They reached the bus stop

just as the school bus _____. They _____ the

handlebar as they got on the bus.

Name _____ **Date** _____

Selection Vocabulary

Focus

porch (pôrch) *n.* an entrance covered with a roof (page 44)

cement (si•ment´) *n.* a mix of sand, water, and rock that dries as hard as stone (page 53)

electrician (i•lek•trish´•ən) *n.* a person who works with wires and electricity (page 56)

hut (hut) *n.* a small plain house (page 40)

Practice Review the vocabulary words and definitions from *Building a House* and *Homes Around the World.* Write two sentences using at least one of the vocabulary words in each sentence.

1. _____

2. _____

Apply

Write the word from the word box that matches each definition below.

hut   porch
electrician   cement

1. _____ : an entrance covered with a roof

2. _____ : a person who works with wires and electricity

3. _____ : a small plain house

4. _____ : a mix of sand, water, and rock that dries as hard as stone

Name _____ **Date** _____

Consonant Blends /st/ and /tr/

Focus

Rule

- Consonant blends join two or more consonants with little change in the individual sounds. Listen carefully for the individual sounds.
- The consonant blend /st/ is spelled **st** and the consonant blend /tr/ is spelled **tr.**

Example
store   **tr**ade

Word List

1. stamp
2. stick
3. steal
4. stay
5. true
6. train
7. track
8. try

Challenge Words

9. stable
10. truly

Practice **Sort the spelling words under the correct heading.**

/st/ spelled *st*

1. _____
2. _____
3. _____
4. _____

/tr/ spelled *tr*

5. _____
6. _____
7. _____
8. _____

Apply Look at each word below. If the word is spelled correctly, write the word *correct* on the line. If the word is misspelled, write the correct spelling on the line.

9. smick _____

10. track _____

11. frue _____

12. smay _____

13. steal _____

14. try _____

15. prack _____

16. frain _____

Write the spelling word on the line next to its meaning clue.

17. take without permission _____

18. not false _____

19. course or path _____

20. to walk heavily or noisily _____

Name _____ **Date** _____

Putting Titles in Alphabetical Order

It is helpful to organize your books in **alphabetical order** when you are doing research. You can organize books by arranging the selections in ABC order, using the first word of the title. If there are several titles that start with the same word, then also look at the second word in the title.

Read the book titles and then write them on the lines in alphabetical order.

How a Seed Grows   Plant that Eat Animals

Green and Growing   Flowers

_____

_____

_____

_____

_____

_____

_____

Apply **Write the titles from the Home Sweet Home Unit in alphabetical order.**

Snail's Pace   The White House   Building a House

Homes   Homes Around the World

Name _____ **Date** _____

Classify and Categorize

Classify and Categorize: As you read, group together things and ideas that are alike.

Read each category. Write the words on the lines under the category in which they belong.

| library | fairy tales | doorknob |
| office | fables | clock |

Kinds of Books

_____

_____

_____

Rooms in a School

_____

_____

_____

Things That are Round

_____

_____

Apply **Read each list. Write the category that best describes the words on the list.**

Summer Clothes   In a Grocery Store
Desert Animals   Happy Things
Winter Clothes   In a Garage
Pet Care

_____

garden hose   rattlesnake

spare tires   scorpion

ladder   tarantula

car   camel

_____

shorts   fresh water

tee shirts   food

swimsuit   keep safe

sandals   hugs

Name _____ **Date** _____

Explaining a Process

Think **Audience: Who** will read your explanation?

_____

_____

Purpose: What do you want your explanation to do?

_____

Prewriting **Complete the sequence map below to help you plan your writing. Use one of the topics from your Writer's Notebooks.**

My Topic _____

First	Next

And then	Finally

Revising **Use this checklist to revise your writing about a process.**

☐ Is your first step at the beginning?

☐ Did you turn each idea into a complete sentence?

☐ Are the steps clear and easy to follow?

☐ Did you move around text that might be out of place in the paragraph?

Editing/Proofreading **Use this checklist to correct mistakes.**

☐ Did you use proofreading marks to help make editing easier?

☐ Are all words spelled correctly?

☐ Did you have a partner read over your writing?

Publishing **Use this checklist to get your writing ready to share.**

☐ Copy your writing on a clean sheet of paper or write it on the computer.

☐ Give your writing a title at the top of the page.

Name _____ **Date** _____

Future Tense Verbs

Rule
Future tense verbs show an action that will happen in the future. It can be formed by using the word *will* with the verb.

Example
I **will finish** my homework tonight.

Practice **Read each sentence. Draw a line under the future tense verb.**

1. Soon they will load the boxes on the truck.

2. We will walk to school tomorrow.

3. Maria will make treats for our picnic next Saturday.

4. Our team will play a game this weekend.

5. The cat will climb up that tree.

6. I will go on a trip.

Apply **Read each sentence. Circle the words that will make it future tense and write them on the line.**

7. Christy's family _____ camping next month.

   will go   went

8. Dad _____ everything the night before they leave. will pack   packed.

9. Mom and Aunt Betty _____ the food ahead of time.   prepared   will prepare

10. Christy and Mark _____ the games to take on the trip.   will plan   planned

11. Mark _____ his cousin will be there.

    hoped   will hope

12. Their dogs Swaggerty and Callie _____ with them.   will travel   traveled

Name _____ **Date** _____

Sounds and Spellings Review

Focus Digraphs are two or more letters that make one sound.

Practice **Read each sentence. Circle the word with the digraph. Write the digraph on the line.**

1. We ate brunch at a new restaurant. _____

2. Dad put milk into a pitcher. _____

3. Bart made a chart about space travel. _____

4. Melinda used clay to shape a bowl. _____

5. We picked fresh strawberries out of our garden. _____

6. Mom and I put family photos in a new album. _____

Apply **Read each riddle. Write the correct word on the line.**

| cheese | alphabet | sunshine | clothing |

7. I make words.

I have vowels and

consonants.

I have 26 letters.

What am I?

_____

_ _ _ _ _ _ _ _ _ _ _ _ _

_____

8. I am food.

I can be yellow or white.

Mice really like me.

What am I?

_____

_ _ _ _ _ _ _ _ _ _ _ _ _

_____

9. You wear me.

I am a shirt.

I am a robe.

What am I?

_____

_ _ _ _ _ _ _ _ _ _ _ _ _

_____

10. You see me a lot in the

summer.

You play out in me.

I come from the sun.

What am I?

_____

_ _ _ _ _ _ _ _ _ _ _ _ _

_____

Name _____ Date _____

Main Idea and Details

Focus Good readers identify the **main idea** and **details** of a selection to help them better understand what is happening.

Practice **Read the main idea and the details. Then circle the sentence that does not belong.**

Main Idea: Weather

Details:

1. The snow was melting in the sunshine.

2. It was so cold that the rain turned into hail.

3. They went swimming in the pool because it was so hot.

4. He had to take a bath because he was covered with dirt.

5. The cool air outside made her nose cold.

6 His mom drove him to school because it was raining.

Apply **Read the main idea. Then circle the words that do not belong.**

Main Idea: Materials used to make shelters

Details:

wood	dirt	grapes
leaves	cement	mud
bricks	nails	cloth
water	sticks	ice
reeds	stones	birds

Name _____ **Date** _____

Consonant digraphs /sh/ and /ch/

Focus

Rule	Example
• Consonant digraphs are consonants next to each other that represent one sound. The sound can be at the beginning or end of a word or syllable. • The consonant digraph /sh/ is spelled *sh* and the consonant digraph /ch/ can be spelled *ch* or ■ *tch*.	**sh**op bun**ch**

Word List

1. ship
2. rich
3. shade
4. teach
5. chalk
6. dish
7. wash
8. check

Challenge Words

9. shadow
10. child

Practice **Sort the spelling words under the correct heading.**

/sh/ spelled *sh.*   /ch/ spelled *ch.*

1. _____   5. _____

2. _____   6. _____

3. _____   7. _____

4. _____   8. _____

Apply **Read each word. If the word is spelled correctly, write *correct* on the line. If the word is misspelled, write the correct spelling.**

9. shalk _____

10. rish _____

11. ship _____

12. teash _____

13. shade _____

14. dish _____

15. sheck _____

16. wach _____

Write the spelling word next to its meaning clue.

17. to look over _____

18. used for marking _____

19. a large vessel for water travel _____

20. shallow container for holding food _____

21. wealthy _____

22. blocking of light rays _____

Name _____ Date _____

Organizing Story Sequence

Focus Writing a **story sequence** is like making a map that shows information from a reading selection. Organizing a story sequence can also help you plan something you are going to write.

Practice **Read each sentence below. Number them in the order they would come in a story.**

_____ First we got out some board games to play.

_____ Finally, the sun came out.

_____ It was a rainy day.

_____ Then we colored pictures with crayons and markers.

_____ We could not play outside.

_____ We put on our jackets and ran through the door.

_____ We decided to play inside.

Apply The story below is written in the wrong order. Read the story and rewrite the sentences so they are in the correct order.

My dad put on the training wheels. It was time to practice riding my bike. I practiced riding up and down the sidewalk. My dad cheered as I took off riding on just two wheels. Then it was time for Dad to take off the training wheels.

_____

_____

_____

_____

_____

_____

_____

Name _____ **Date** _____

Selection Vocabulary

Focus

trudge (truj) *v.* to walk slowly with heavy steps (page 82)

famous (fā´•məs) *adj.* well known (page 77)

president (prez´•i•dənt) *n.* the leader of the United States (page 67)

Practice **Write the word from the word box that completes each sentence.**

I. Bill had to _____ through deep snow to get to school.

2. The _____ lives and works in the White House.

3. The Golden Gate Bridge is a _____ bridge.

Apply Tell whether the boldface definition that is given for the underlined word in each sentence below makes sense. Circle Yes or No.

> trudge   famous   president

4. The <u>president</u> greeted visitors in the East Room.

watching   Yes   No

5. Dave had to <u>trudge</u> up the stairs with the heavy box.

sitting   Yes   No

6. Have you read about the most <u>famous</u> home in America?

well known   Yes   No

Name _____ **Date** _____

Timed Writing

Think   **Audience: Who** will read your timed writing?

_____

Purpose: What do you want your timed writing to do?

_____

_____

_____

Prewriting   **Follow these steps for timed writing.**

I. Read the entire prompt. Circle the directions for writing the paper.

2. Underline each thing you are asked to write about.

3. Reread each reminder.

4. Make notes about what you will write. Spend only a few minutes.

5. Write your paper!

6. Check to make sure you did each reminder.

7. Revise as needed.

Revising | **Use this checklist to make your timed writing better.**

☐ Did you complete each reminder?

☐ Does your writing stay on topic?

☐ Are your sentences clear?

Editing/Proofreading | **Use this checklist to check your timed writing.**

☐ Did you begin every sentence with a capital letter?

☐ Did you use correct end marks?

☐ Are all words spelled correctly?

Name _____ **Date** _____

Singular, Plural, and Possessive Nouns

Focus	Rule Add **'s** to a noun or name to show ownership.	Example Jake**'s** hat the dog**'s** tail

Practice A **Read each sentence. Draw a line under the singular nouns. Circle the plural nouns. Draw a box around the possessive nouns.**

1. The kittens slept on the chair.

2. Janet put the dishes in the sink.

3. Burt's horse galloped to the gate.

Practice B **Read the sentence. Circle the correct word and write it on the line.**

1. The _____ water dish tipped over.

    dog   dog's   dogs

Singular, Plural, and Possessive Pronouns

Focus	Rule	Example
	A **possessive pronoun** takes the place of a possessive noun. It shows ownership.	Tammy's shoes are black. **Her** shoes are black.

Practice A   Read each sentence. Draw a line under the singular pronouns. Circle the plural pronouns. Draw a box around the possessive pronouns.

1. Jessie and I raked their leaves.

2. We played the big drums in the parade.

Practice B   Rewrite the sentence to change the underlined nouns to pronouns.

3. Kathy's book is in Mike's desk.

_____

Name _____ **Date** _____

Sounds and Spellings Review

Practice A Read each category. Write the words that belong under each category.

| snarl | drummer | burro | storyteller |
| horns | partridge | slurp | teacher |

People
_____
- - - - - - - - - - - -
_____
- - - - - - - - - - - -
_____

Sounds
_____
- - - - - - - - - - - -
_____
- - - - - - - - - - - -
_____

A Parade
_____
- - - - - - - - - - - -
_____
- - - - - - - - - - - -
_____

Animals
_____
- - - - - - - - - - - -
_____
- - - - - - - - - - - -
_____

Practice B

swirled   shore   surrounded   storm

There would not be a _____ at the coast today. We

walked along the sandy _____. Cool little waves

_____ around our feet. We laughed as the seagulls

_____ the breadcrumbs that we tossed on the sand.

Name _____ **Date** _____

Compare and Contrast

You will better understand and keep track of what you read if you identify things within the selection that are **alike** and **different**.

Practice A Compare and contrast a car and a pickup truck. Tell how each is different. Then tell how they are alike.

seatbelts	open in back	shorter

 Car

Truck

_____   _____

_____   _____

A car and a truck are alike.

_____

_____

Practice B **Read each description. At the bottom, tell how the objects are different and how they are alike.**

Crayons are made of wax. Crayons come in many colors. You can use a crayon to draw a picture.

Pencils are made of wood. Pencils make black marks. They have erasers so you can correct mistakes. You hold a pencil in your hand. You can use a pencil to draw a picture.

Crayon   **Alike**   **Pencil**

_____   _____   _____

_____   _____   _____

_____   _____   _____

Name _____ **Date** _____

R-controlled Vowels

Focus

Rule	Example
R-controlled vowels make a special sound. The r-controlled vowel sound /ar/ spelling is **ar** and the r-controlled vowel sound /or/ spelling is **or.**	m**ar**k w**or**n

Word List
1. park
2. cart
3. order
4. core
5. store
6. torn
7. hard
8. harm

Challenge Words
9. garden
10. story

Practice A **Sort the spelling words under the correct heading.**

/ar/ spelled *ar*

1. _____

2. _____

3. _____

4. _____

/or/ spelled *or*

5. _____

6. _____

7. _____

8. _____

Practice B | Beside each word, write the spelling word that rhymes on the line.

9. yard _____

10. more _____

11. start _____

12. farm _____

13. worn _____

14. border _____

15. dark _____

16. sore _____

Name _____ **Date** _____

Selection Vocabulary

Focus

creatures
(krē´•chərz) *n.*
Plural of **creature:**
a living person or
animal (page 91)
hibernating
(hī´•bər•nāt´•ing)
v. Form of the verb
hibernate: to sleep
through the winter
(page 94)

shady (shā´•dē) *adj.*
giving shade; blocking
out light (page 96)
comfort (kum´•fərt)
n. a good feeling;
having what you need
(page 110)

Practice A **Write the word from the word box**
that completes each sentence.

I. The bear left the den after _____ for many weeks.

2. Dan found a _____ spot in the yard.

3. We came in from the cold to enjoy the _____ of a warm room.

4. Many _____ in the desert are active at night.

Practice B **Write the word from the word box that matches each definition below.**

> hibernating   shady
>
> comfort   creatures

5. _____ blocking out light

6. _____ living people or animals

7. _____ sleeping through the winter

8. _____ a good feeling; having what you need

Name _____ **Date** _____

Writing an Opinion Statement

Think **Audience: Who** will read your statement?

_____

_____

Purpose: What do you want your opinion statement to do?

_____

_____

Prewriting **Complete the web below to help get ideas for your opinion statement. Remember to focus on the question:** _Which kind of house would be more fun to live in, a tree house or a house boat?_

Revising **Use this checklist to revise your opinion statement.**

☐ Does every sentence tell about your opinion on the question?

☐ Did you add descriptive details and re-write unclear sentences in your sentences?

☐ Did you explain your opinion to a partner to come up with ideas for your writing?

Editing/Proofreading **Use this checklist to correct mistakes.**

☐ Did you choose the correct tense for the verbs in your writing?

☐ Did you edit your writing with a partner to help find your mistakes?

Publishing **Use this checklist to get your report ready to share.**

☐ Copy your opinion statement on a clean sheet of paper.

Name _____ **Date** _____

Selection Vocabulary

> **Focus**   **tunnels**   **shared** (shârd) *v.*
>
> (tun´•əlz) *n.*   Past tense of **share:**
>
> Plural of **tunnel:**   to divide with others
>
> an underground   (page 135)
>
> passageway
>
> (page 123)

Practice A   **Circle the correct word that completes the sentence.**

1. The ants lived in sandy _____ under the grass.

    a. different   **b.** turning   **c.** tunnels

2. My brother and I _____ a room for two years.

    a. shady   **b.** shared   **c.** storm

Practice B Review the vocabulary words and definitions from *This House Is Made of Mud.* Write two sentences using at least one of the vocabulary words in each sentence.

1. _____

_____

2. _____

_____

Name _____ **Date** _____

Past, Present, and Future Verbs Review

Practice A   **Read each sentence. Circle the verb.
Then write an X under the correct column
to tell if the verb is the past, present, or future tense.**

	Past	Present	Future
1. Lindsey giggles at everyone's jokes.	_____	_____	_____
2. We spent hours washing the car.	_____	_____	_____
3. Bob and Jim will play soccer next spring.	_____	_____	_____
4. The playful kittens pounce on each other.	_____	_____	_____
5. Laura will play the piano this summer.	_____	_____	_____
6. Ryan rides the bus to day camp.	_____	_____	_____

Practice B   **Read each sentence. Circle the verb that correctly completes each sentence and write it on the line.**

7. I am _____ to the dentist tomorrow.

   go   going   gone

8. Mr. Dalmane will _____ new toys for next year.

   make   making   made

9. Julian _____ the books to the library last week.

   return   returning   returned

10. Sharon _____ rope all recess.

   jumps   jumping   jumped

11. Last night the wind _____ very hard.

   blows   blowing   blew

12. Brad and Marv are _____ dad clean out the garage.

   help   helping   helped

Name _____ Date _____

Sounds and Spellings Review

Name each picture clue. Write the word in the puzzle.

cartwheel	sweatshirt	toothbrush	pitcher
melon	tractor	thermometer	grapes

Across

1.
3.
4.
5.

Down

1.
2.
6.
7.

Sounds and Spellings Review

Write the missing word to complete each sentence.

8. We ate bread and honey for _____.
   breakfast butter

9. He laid a _____ carpet over the hard floor.
   cloudy heavy

10. Mr. Davis went to the _____ to pick up my grandfather.
    airplane airport

11. Steven _____ for his dog Cosmo to come.
    whistled rang

12. Trisha stacked three _____ on the shelf.
    cartoons cartons

13. Tyler dug a bigger hole in the _____ before he added more seeds.
    dirt down

Name _____ Date _____

Making Inferences

Making Inferences is using what you already know to help answer questions while reading.

Practice A   **Read the paragraph. Read the questions. Draw an X on the line in front of the correct answer. Then follow the directions.**

The bell rang. All of us quickly put our pencils and papers in our desks. We listened for our row to be called. Then we quietly put on our jackets and lined up at the room door. We walked down the hallway and out the doors. The air felt a little chilly. A few of us hurried to the swings. Others ran to the slides. Some just started chasing each other.

1. Where are the children?

_____ at summer camp   _____ at school

Draw a line under the words in the paragraph that tell you this.

Practice B   Using the story from page 183, answer the questions below. Draw an X on the line in front of the correct answer. Then follow the directions.

2. What time of year is it?

_____ hot summer   _____ fall

Circle the words in the paragraph that tell you this.

3. What are the children doing?

_____ having recess   _____ eating lunch

Draw a box around the words that tell you this.

Name _____ **Date** _____

Consonant Digraphs /hw/ and /th/

Focus

Rule	Example
Consonant digraphs are two consonants next to each other that represent one sound. The consonant digraph /hw/ is spelled **wh** and the consonant digraph /th/ is spelled **th.**	**wh**at **th**ick

Word List
1. path
2. three
3. birth
4. white
5. whale
6. throw
7. whim
8. while

Challenge Words
9. whistle
10. thought

Practice A **Sort the spelling words under the correct heading.**

/hw/ spelled *wh*

1. _____
2. _____
3. _____
4. _____

/th/ spelled *th*

5. _____
6. _____
7. _____
8. _____

Practice B **Beside each word, write the spelling word that rhymes.**

9. kite _____

10. mirth _____

11. show _____

12. sale _____

Write the spelling word next to its meaning clue.

13. a sudden idea or impulse _____

14. a track or trail _____

15. a period of time _____

16. a number _____

Name _____ **Date** _____

Persuasive Writing

Think **Audience: Who** will read your persuasive poster?

_____

_____

Purpose: What do you want your persuasive poster about fear to do?

_____

_____

Prewriting **Brainstorm ideas to use for your poster below.**

I. What things are you afraid of?

_____

2. What are some ways that you can overcome your fears?

_____

On another sheet of paper draw a picture of what your poster might look like.

Revising **Use this checklist to make your poster better.**

☐ Does your poster help readers want to think, feel or do something about facing a fear?

☐ Does your poster tell about what you are afraid of and how you can deal with that fear?

Editing/Proofreading **Use this checklist to correct mistakes.**

☐ Did you begin every sentence with a capital letter?

☐ Did you use correct end marks?

☐ Are all words spelled correctly?

Publishing **Use this checklist to get your persuasive poster ready to share.**

☐ Did you add a picture or photo to your poster?

☐ Does your poster have a title?

Name _____ **Date** _____

Adjectives, Synonyms, and Antonyms

Rule	Examples		
Adjectives are describing words that tell more about something.	bright	brighter	brightest

Practice A **Read each sentence. Circle the adjective. Write an X on the line to tell if it compares two or more than two.**

	Compares 2	Compares More Than 2
1. Chad is the fastest runner on our team.	_____	_____
2. The blue rope is longer than the red one.	_____	_____
3. This cracker is the crunchiest I ever ate.	_____	_____
4. Mrs. Garcia's oak tree is older than ours.	_____	_____

Practice B   Read the word pairs. Write S if they mean the same. Write O if they mean the opposite.

5. subtract   add   _____

6. fix   repair   _____

7. plump   fat   _____

8. healthy   sick   _____

9. full   empty   _____

Read each sentence. Circle the word that correctly completes the sentence. Write the word on the line.

10. Carla keeps her bedroom neat and _____.

    tidy   messy

11. The puppy is not strong enough to walk on its _____ baby legs.

    powerful   weak

Name _____ **Date** _____

Sounds and Spellings Review

Unscramble the letters and write the word on the line. Find and circle the word in the puzzle.

```
c  f  s  c  o  o  p  b  a
s  a  l  u  t  e  j  o  b
m  s  i  b  n  g  d  o  u
e  c  p  r  u  n  e  t  g
n  r  e  t  u  l  i  p  l
u  e  k  h  t  u  b  a  e
x  w  j  e  w  e  l  r  y
```

1. c w e s r _____

2. n u r p e _____

3. a u t b _____

4. a u t e s l _____

5. n m u e _____

6. p u i t l _____

7. o b o t _____

8. o s p c o _____

Sounds and Spellings Review

Practice B **Look at the picture. Read each sentence. Write the word that rhymes with the underlined word and makes sense to complete each sentence.**

| stew | mule | spoon | brook | goose |

9. It is no <u>use</u> to try to catch that _____.

10. He can play a <u>tune</u> with a _____.

11. The <u>rule</u> is to keep the _____ in the pen.

12. Is it <u>true</u> dad makes a great _____?

13. <u>Look</u> at all the fish in the _____!

Name _____ Date _____

Vocabulary

Focus

underneath (un´
• dər • nēth´) *adv.*
below (page 150)

beards (bērdz) *n.* Plural
of **beard:** the hair that
grows on a man's face
(page 151)

clenched (klencht) *v.*
Past tense of **clench:**
to close tightly (page
166)

trembling (trem´ • bəl
• ing) *v.* shaking (page
166)

Practice A   **Write the word from the word box that completes each sentence.**

I. Maria _____ her fist around her lunch money.

2. Jeff tried to look brave, but his hands were _____.

3. Our dog took my shoe _____ my bed to chew it.

4. Many presidents of the United States wore _____.

Practice B **Write the word from the word box that matches each definition below.**

underneath   trembling
beards   clenched

5. _____ the hair that grows on a man's face

6. _____ to close tightly

7. _____ below

8. _____ shaking

Vocabulary • *Skills Practice 2*

Name _____ **Date** _____

/o͞o/ spelled *oo* and /oo/ spelled *oo*

Focus

Rule
The short /oo/spelling is *oo*. One spelling for long /o͞o/is *oo*.

Examples
m**oo**d   t**oo**k

Practice A

Sort the spelling words and write them under the correct heading.

Word List
1. droop
2. book
3. good
4. noon
5. moose
6. food
7. shook
8. wood

Challenge Words
9. balloon
10. wooden

/o͞o/ spelled *oo*

1. _____

2. _____

3. _____

4. _____

/oo/ spelled *oo*

5. _____

6. _____

7. _____

8. _____

Practice B   **Beside each compound word, write the spelling word that it contains.**

9. cookbook _____

10. good-bye _____

11. firewood _____

12. seafood _____

Write the spelling word next to its meaning clue.

13. middle of the day _____

14. to bend or hang down _____

15. material from trees _____

16. a hoofed mammal _____

Name _____ **Date** _____

Alphabetical Order

Focus Fiction books are placed on shelves in **alphabetical order**. The librarian places these books on shelves according to the author's last name. The first letter of the author's last name is used in alphabetical order.

Practice A Underline the first letter of the author's last name. Put these letters in alphabetical order at the bottom of the page.

Allan Fowler

Chieri Uegaki

Arnold Lobel

Lois Osborn

Deborah Eaton

_____ _____ _____ _____ _____

_____ _____ _____ _____ _____

Practice B | **Write the author's names on the lines in alphabetical order.**

Margaret Clark

_____

Bernard Waber

_____

Marc Brown

_____

Robin Nelson

_____

Joan Sweeney

_____

Name _____ **Date** _____

Drawing Conclusions

Readers **draw conclusions** by taking small pieces of information about a character or story event and use the information to guess something about the character or event.

Look at each picture. Then answer each question. Circle your answers.

1. How does Christy feel?

   a. sad   **b.** proud

2. Why does she feel this way?

   a. She grew the biggest pumpkin.

   b. The judge is smiling.

   c. She is at the fair.

Practice B   **Read the story. Answer each question with an X. Follow the directions under each question.**

Pam rubbed her hands while looking up and down the street. She pulled her coat around her and put her hands in her pockets. Sitting on the bench, Pam shivered and waited.

3. Where is Pam?   inside _____   outside _____

Draw a line under the words in the story that tell you this.

4. What is it like outside?   cold _____   warm _____

Draw circles around the words in the story that tell you this.

Name _____ **Date** _____

Writing a Summary

Think   **Audience: Who** will read your summary?

_____

_____

Purpose: Why is it important to be able to write a summary?

_____

_____

Prewriting   **Plan your summary by completing the outline below.**

Main Characters: _____

List two important things that happen in the story.

• _____

• _____

How did the story end?

• _____

Revising **Use this list to help make your summary better.**

☐ Do the sentences of your summary have different lengths so that they do not all sound the same?

☐ Does your summary have a beginning, a middle, and an end?

☐ Did you remember to include the story's title and author at the top of the summary?

Editing/Proofreading **Use this checklist to correct mistakes in your summary.**

☐ Did you use capital letters and end marks correctly?

☐ Are all words spelled correctly?

Publishing **Use this checklist to get your summary ready to share.**

☐ Copy your summary on a clean sheet of paper.

Name _____ **Date** _____

Types of Sentences

Telling sentences tell a thought and end with a period. **Asking sentences** ask a question and end with a question mark.

Practice A **Draw a line under the telling sentences. Circle the asking sentences.**

I. Which one can we go on first?

2. I want to ride on the brown horse.

3. Do you think Bill can hit the target?

4. I had a fun day at the park.

Types of Sentences

Focus **Strong-feeling** sentences show surprise or excitement and end with an exclamation point. **Imperative** sentences give a command and can end with a period or exclamation point.

Practice A

Write two strong feeling sentences about the picture.

_____

_____

Write command sentences about the picture.

_____

_____

Name _____ **Date** _____

Sounds and Spellings Review

Practice A Read the headings. Write the words under the category where they belong.

growl	browse	owl	towel	shout	hound
pouch	pounce	howl	point	oyster	soil

Animals
_____
_____
_____
_____

Things You Can Do
_____
_____
_____
_____

Sounds
_____
_____
_____
_____

Things You Can Hold
_____
_____
_____
_____

Practice B   **Write the correct word to complete the sentences in the story.**

> crown town loud crowd
> gown loyal tower

The queen heard _____ cheers. She put on her purple

velvet _____ and jeweled _____.

She went to look out a window in the _____.

Below she saw a large _____. The people of the

_____ would always be _____ to her.

Name _____ **Date** _____

Diphthongs /ow/ spelled *ou_* and /oi/ spelled *oi*

Focus

Rule
The /ow/ sound can be spelled *ou_*, and the /oi/ sound can be spelled *oi*. The /ow/ and /oi/ sounds are made by making a gradual movement from one vowel sound to the next vowel sound.

Example
r**ou**nd   c**oi**l

Word List

1. sound
2. couch
3. boil
4. house
5. soil
6. loud
7. coin
8. noise

Challenge Words

9. around
10. joined

Practice A
Sort the spelling words under the correct heading.

/ow/ spelled *ou_*   /oi/ spelled *oi*

1. _____   5. _____

2. _____   6. _____

3. _____   7. _____

4. _____   8. _____

Practice B **Circle the correct spelling for each word. Write the correct spelling on the line.**

9. soind   sound   _____

10. boil   boyl   _____

11. coin   coyn   _____

12. howse   house   _____

Write the spelling word that rhymes with each word.

13. coil   _____

14. pouch   _____

15. cloud   _____

16. poise   _____

Name _____ **Date** _____

Organizing Story Sequence

Organizing a story's sequence is a way to map what has happened in a story. A story sequence, or outline, can also be used to help you plan something you are going to write.

Practice A **Write sentences that describe action in the last story we read, "My Brother Is Afraid of Just About Everything." You may refer back to _Student Reader 2_ to review details from the story.**

_____

_____

_____

_____

_____

_____

Practice B

Create a story sequence by writing the sentences from the story in the correct order.

1. _____

2. _____

3. _____

4. _____

5. _____

6. _____

7. _____

8. _____

Name _____ Date _____

Vocabulary

Focus

thrill (thril) *n.* a feeling of excitement (page 189)

peeking (pēk´ • ing) *v.* looking quickly or secretly (page 203)

solo (sō´ • lō) *n.* music that one person sings or plays on an instrument (page 191)

sneaking (snēk´ • ing) *v.* moving or acting quietly, secretly (page 203)

Practice A   **Write the word from the word box that matches each definition below.**

peeking	solo
thrill	sneaking

1. _____ looking quickly or secretly

2. _____ a feeling of excitement

3. _____ moving or acting quietly, secretly

4. _____ music that one person sings or plays on an instrument

Practice B **Circle the correct word that completes the sentence.**

5. We heard Lee play a _____ on his flute.

a. hen   **b.** solo   **c.** walking

6. Dad and I were _____ into the crib to see the sleeping baby.

a. peeking   **b.** solo   **c.** weekend

7. My mom enjoys the _____ of riding a roller coaster.

a. voice   **b.** cute   **c.** thrill

8. A cat was _____ past the door without a sound.

a. sneaking   **b.** flower   **c.** smooth

Name _____ **Date** _____

Writing a Fable

Think   **Audience: Who** will read your fable?

_____

_____

Purpose: What do you want your fable to do?

_____

_____

Prewriting   **Use the story map to plan your fable.**

Beginning

Middle

End

Revising **Use this checklist to make your fable better.**

☐ Does your fable have a title?

☐ Does your fable have talking animals?

☐ Is there a problem in your fable that is solved in the end?

☐ Does your fable have a moral or teach a lesson?

Editing/Proofreading **Use this checklist to check your fable.**

☐ Did you begin every sentence with a capital letter and end it with the correct end mark?

☐ Are all words spelled correctly?

☐ Did you have a peer edit your fable?

Publishing **Use this checklist to get your fable ready to publish.**

☐ Copy your fable on a clean sheet of paper or type it on the computer.

☐ Draw an illustration to go with your fable.

Writing • *Skills Practice 2*

Name _____ **Date** _____

Reality and Fantasy

In **reality stories,** characters talk and act like real people, and the events could happen in real life. In **fantasy stories,** the main characters are often animals that talk and behave like people. Fantasy stories could never happen in real life.

Practice A **Read each sentence below. If it is an example of reality, write** *reality* **on the line. If it is an example of fantasy, write** *fantasy* **on the line.**

1. Bob the beaver asked his friend Tom the tuna to help him build a home for his family.

   _____

   - - - - - - - - - -

2. Jill wanted a new sweater. She asked her mom if she could earn money by doing extra chores.

   _____

   - - - - - - - - - -

Practice B | Circle **Reality** or **Fantasy.**

3. Eddie and Sam put up the tent.   Reality   Fantasy

4. Leo Leopard yelled, "I'm going to jog to the park."   Reality   Fantasy

5. The pig carefully drove the tractor to the cornfield.   Reality   Fantasy

6. Rusty walks his dog Dusty every day.   Reality   Fantasy

7. Wanda Wolf read a bedtime story to her cubs.   Reality   Fantasy

8. Rachel helped Mom fold the clean clothes.   Reality   Fantasy

Comprehension • *Skills Practice 2*

Name _____ Date _____

Capitalization

Focus | **Rule**

Use a **capital letter** for the first word of a sentence, the pronoun I, cities and states, names of special people, places, and things, days of the week, and the months.

Practice A **Read each sentence. Draw a line under the words that should begin with a capital letter. Write the correct capital letter above the word.**

1. miguel lives in madrid, spain.

2. his family will visit us in june.

3. it is a long trip to seaside, oregon.

4. we want to show them the sea lion caves.

**Read each sentence.
Write the sentence
correctly on the line.**

5. the new portsmouth zoo opened the first monday in july.

_____

_____

6. my family and i want to see the baby pandas.

_____

_____

7. our friends mrs. selvin and paula will go with us.

_____

_____

Name _____ **Date** _____

Word Building

Practice A Read each word.
Circle the base word.
Draw a line under the prefix and/or word ending.

1. blushed

2. smarter

3. darting

4. quietness

5. higher

6. disappear

7. unfeeling

8. chores

9. untrue

10. pecking

11. weeded

12. disinfected

13. plainness

14. unfinished

FINISH

Practice B **Read each sentence.**

Write the correct prefix or word ending to complete the word.

un	dis	er	est
s	ing	ed	ness

15. Kim zoom_____ out the door.

16. Mom was _____pleased that the puppy had chew_____ the mat.

17. Nan was _____afraid of exploring the cave.

18. Mr. Chin was water_____ his flower_____.

19. The thick_____ of the jacket made it too bulky.

20. Jane writes the neat_____ papers in the class.

21. Kayla can do math problems quick_____ than Steven.

22. Mr. Bailey _____lock_____ the door.

Name _____ **Date** _____

Vocabulary

Focus

usually (ū´•zhōō•əl•ē) *adv.* most of the time (page 211)

clumsy (klum´•zē) *adj.* awkward; not graceful (page 213)

suggest (səg•jest´) *v.* to give or tell an idea (page 227)

excitement (ik•sīt´•mənt) *n.* a mood or feeling of high interest or energy; delight; joy (page 228)

Practice A
Match each word on the left to its definition on the right.

l. suggest

2. usually

3. excitement

4. clumsy

a. awkward, not graceful

b. a mood or feeling of high interest or energy; delight; joy

c. to give or tell an idea

d. most of the time

Practice B Tell whether the boldface definition that is given for the underlined word in each sentence below makes sense. Circle Yes or No.

1. I am going to <u>suggest</u> we go for a walk after dinner.
quickly   Yes   No

2. Emily <u>usually</u> rides the bus to go downtown.
never   Yes   No

3. Rico decided to practice skating so he would not feel <u>clumsy</u> on the ice.
awkward   Yes   No

4. The <u>excitement</u> of the birthday party lasted all afternoon.
feeling of high energy   Yes   No

Name _____ **Date** _____

Word Endings –s and –ed

Focus

Rules	Examples
• The common ending spelled **–s** means more than one or an action that is happening right now.	The cat sit**s**. The other cat**s** run.
• The common ending spelled **–ed** means that something has already happened. It can make the /ed/ sound, /d/ sound, or /t/ sound.	end**ed** color**ed** bak**ed**

Word List

1. likes
2. liked
3. opens
4. opened
5. parts
6. parted
7. chases
8. chased

Challenge Words

9. buried
10. exclaimed

Practice A

Sort the spelling words and write them under the correct heading.

ending spelled -s   ending spelled -ed

1. _____   5. _____

2. _____   6. _____

3. _____   7. _____

4. _____   8. _____

Practice B   **Look at each word below. If the word is spelled correctly, write the word *correct* on the line. If the word is misspelled, write the correct spelling on the line.**

9. chasez _____

10. opend _____

11. likes _____

12. chased _____

13. partd _____

14. likd _____

15. partes _____

Write the spelling words that complete each word family.

16. like _____ _____

17. part _____ _____

18. open _____ _____

19. chase _____ _____

Spelling • *Skills Practice 2*

Name _____ **Date** _____

Alphabetical Order

It is helpful to organize your books in **alphabetical order** when you are doing research. Then, it is easy to find the title you are looking for without having to remember the author's name.

Practice A **Underline the first word in each of the book titles. Then put the books in alphabetical order.**

Suki's Kimono   *Red-Eyed Tree Frog*

Back to School   *Zinnia's Flower Garden*

1. _____

2. _____

3. _____

4. _____

Practice B

Write the title of four books from your classroom in alphabetical order.

1. _____

2. _____

3. _____

4. _____

Name _____ **Date** _____

Writing a Realistic Story

Think   Audience: **Who** will read your story?

_____

_____

Purpose: **What** do you want your story to do?

_____

_____

Prewriting   **Use the story map to plan your story.**

Beginning

Middle

End

Revising Use this checklist to make your story better.

☐ Does your story have a title?

☐ Does your story tell about a problem and how it was solved?

☐ Does your story use describing words and action words?

Editing/Proofreading Use this checklist to check your story.

☐ Did you begin every sentence with a capital letter and end it with the correct end mark?

☐ Are all words spelled correctly?

☐ Did you write contractions correctly in your story?

Publishing Use this checklist to get your story ready to publish.

☐ Copy your story on a clean sheet of paper or write it on the computer.

Name _____ Date _____

Selection Vocabulary

Focus

problem (prob´ • ləm) *n.* a difficulty; a tricky or uncomfortable situation (page 239)

match (mach) *n.* a contest or game (page 244)

changed mind (chānjd mīnd) *v.* Past tense of **change mind:** to go back on a decision (page 262)

Practice A Review the vocabulary words and definitions from *Ira Sleeps Over.*
Write two sentences using at least one of the vocabulary words in each sentence.

1. _____

   _____

2. _____

   _____

Write the word from the word box that completes each sentence.

problem   match   changed mind

1. At first Nick wanted to play outside, but then he

_____ _____

_____ his _____.

2. The icy roads caused a _____ for the drivers.

3. Ira and his friend had a wrestling _____.

Name _____ **Date** _____

Contractions

Focus A **contraction** is when two words are combined to make one word.

Practice A **Write the contraction on the line. Use an apostrophe (') to show where letters are missing.**

1. I am   _____

2. was not   _____

3. she is   _____

4. you will   _____

5. we have   _____

Practice B Read each sentence. Circle the two words that can make a contraction. Write the contraction on the line.

6. I am going to camp soon.

_____

7. Mark said he is going also.

_____

8. It is going to be hot there.

_____

9. We will need to pack shorts.

_____

10. I had better start packing.

_____

11. They have planned many fun things for us to do.

_____

12. We are going to have fun!

_____

Name _____ Date _____

Sounds and Spellings Review

Write the correct word in the puzzle that names each picture.

| tray | robot | honey | rainbow |
| night | flute | window | money |

Across

3.

4.

6.

8.

Down

1.

2.

5.

7.

Sounds and Spellings Review

Read the sentences. Circle the words with long vowel sounds. Write them under the correct letter sound.

1. Sam drew nine names out of the huge jar.

2. Grandma can weave a rug.

3. Many cars travel along this road.

A a

E e

I i

O o

U u

Name _____ Date _____

Main Idea and Details

Focus Good readers stop to identify the **main idea and details** of the story to help them better understand what is happening.

Practice A **Read the main idea. Then circle the sentence that does not belong.**

Main Idea: Trying new things can be exciting.

1. I wanted to learn how to ride a two-wheel bike.

2. My aunt took me to the store to buy a bike helmet.

3. I was afraid I might fall off.

4. Cats can be friendly animals.

5. I was brave when I started peddling.

6. It was exciting when I took off by myself!

Main Idea and Details

Practice B	**Read the main idea. Then circle the words that do not belong.**

Main Idea: Going to summer camp is fun.

Details:

cabins	tigers	elephant
trees	hiking	campfire
singing	friends	crafts
lobster	counselors	games
swimming	boats	whale

Name _____   **Date** _____

Word Ending *-ing*

Focus

Rule
The ending spelled **-ing** is added when the base word ends in a consonant. If the base word ends in the letter e, the letter e is dropped before adding the ending spelled *-ing*.

Examples
walk → walk**ing**
ride → rid**ing**

Word List
1. pointing
2. looking
3. hoping
4. walking
5. biking
6. chasing
7. hiding
8. eating

Challenge Words
9. shrinking
10. hearing

Practice A   **Sort the spelling words and write them under the correct heading.**

ending spelled *-ing*

1. _____

2. _____

3. _____

4. _____

ending spelled *-ing* after dropping final e

5. _____

6. _____

7. _____

8. _____

Practice B **Look at each word below. Write the spelling word that is in the same word family on the line.**

9. chase

_____

10. eat

_____

11. point

_____

12. hide

_____

13. walk

_____

14. look

_____

15. hope

_____

16. bike

_____